Scriptural
Stations of the Cross

and Meditations on the Passion of Christ

CHARLES MICHAEL

GIFTED BOOKS AND MEDIA

Copyright

Compiled by Charles Michael

Printed in the United States of America

Paperback ISBN: 978-1-947343-09-2

Gifted Books and Media
Published by Jayclad Publishing LLC
www.giftedbookstore.com

Table of Contents

Note to the Reader

- It is a good practice to recite the Stations of the Cross on a weekly basis (or daily) even outside of lent

- God's Word is alive and active, and it works in us when we whole heartedly meditate on it

- Scripture verses in this book are to be recited by all, if the stations are prayed in a community

- The prayers in this book can be recited either individually or in a community

- There are two versions of scriptural Stations of the Cross (longer and shorter version) given in this book

Scriptural Stations of the Cross

(Longer Version)

*Based on the stations celebrated by Pope John
Paul II on Good Friday 1991*

Opening Prayer:

Leader: My Lord, Jesus Christ, You have made this journey to die for me with unspeakable love; and I have so many times ungratefully abandoned You. But now I love You with all my heart; and, because I love You, I am sincerely sorry for ever having offended You. Pardon me, my God, and permit me to accompany You on this journey. You go to die for love of me; I want, my beloved Redeemer, to die for love of You. My Jesus, I will live and die always united to You.

At the cross her station keeping
Stood the mournful Mother weeping
Close to Jesus to the last

The First Station

Jesus in the Garden of Gethsemane

Our Father...

Jesus went with them to a garden, which is called Gethsemane; and he said to his disciples, "Sit down here, while I go there and pray." (Matt 26:37)
Hail Mary...

Taking with him Peter and the two sons of Zebedee, he began to be sorrowful and saddened. Then he said to them: "My soul is sorrowful, even unto death. Stay here and keep vigil with me." (Matt 26:37-38)
Hail Mary...

Continuing on a little further, he fell prostrate on his face, praying and saying: "My Father, if it is possible, let this chalice pass away from me. Yet truly, let it not be as I will, but as you will." (Matt 26:39)
Hail Mary...

He approached his disciples and found them sleeping. And he said to Peter: "So, were you not able to keep vigil with me for one hour? Be vigilant and pray, so that you may not enter into temptation. Indeed, the spirit is willing, but the flesh is weak." (Matt 26:40-41)
Hail Mary...

Again, a second time, he went and prayed, saying, "My Father, if this chalice cannot pass away, unless I drink it, let your will be

done." And again, he went and found them sleeping, for their eyes were heavy. (Matt 26:42-43)
Hail Mary…

Leaving them behind, again he went and prayed for the third time, saying the same words. (Matt 26:44)
Hail Mary…

Then he approached his disciples and said to them: "Sleep now and rest. Behold, the hour has drawn near, and the Son of man will be delivered into the hands of sinners. Rise up; let us go. Behold, he who will betray me draws near." (Matt 26:45-46)
Hail Mary…

Glory Be…

> *Through her heart, His sorrow sharing*
> *All His bitter anguish bearing*
> *Now at length the sword has passed*

The Second Station

Jesus, Betrayed by Judas, is Arrested

Leader: We adore you, O Christ, and we bless you.

All: Because by your holy cross, you have redeemed the world.

Our Father...

While he was still speaking, behold, Judas, one of the twelve, arrived, and with him was a large crowd with swords and clubs, sent from the leaders of the priests and the elders of the people. (Matt 26:47)
Hail Mary...

He who betrayed him gave them a sign, saying: "Whomever I will kiss, it is he. Take hold of him." And quickly drawing close to Jesus, he said, "Hail, Master." And he kissed him. (Matt 26:48-49)
Hail Mary...

Jesus said to him, "Friend, for what purpose have you come?" Then they approached, and they put their hands on Jesus, and they arrested him. (Matt 26:50)
Hail Mary...

Behold, one of those who were with Jesus, extending his hand, drew his sword and struck the servant of the high priest, cutting off his ear. Then Jesus said to him: "Put your sword back in its place. For all who take up the sword shall perish by the sword." (Matt 26:51-52)
Hail Mary...

Do you think that I cannot ask my Father, so that he would give me, even now, more than twelve legions of angels? How then

would the Scriptures be fulfilled, which say that it must be so?" (Matt 26:53-54)
Hail Mary...

In that same hour, Jesus said to the crowds: "You went out, as if to a robber, with swords and clubs to seize me. Yet I sat daily with you, teaching in the temple, and you did not take hold of me. (Matt 26:55)
Hail Mary...

But all this has happened so that the Scriptures of the prophets may be fulfilled." Then all the disciples fled, abandoning him. (Matt 26:56)
Hail Mary...

Glory Be...

> *O, how sad and sore depressed*
> *Was that Mother highly blessed*
> *Of the sole Begotten One*

The Third Station

Jesus is Condemned by the Sanhedrin

Leader: We adore you, O Christ, and we bless you.

All: Because by your holy cross, you have redeemed the world.

Our Father...

Those who were holding Jesus led him to Caiaphas, the high priest, where the scribes and the elders had joined together. (Matt 26:58)
Hail Mary...

Then the leaders of the priests and the entire council sought false testimony against Jesus, so that they might deliver him to death. And they did not find any, even though many false witnesses had come forward. (Matt 26:59-60)
Hail Mary...

Then, at the very end, two false witnesses came forward and they said, "This man said: 'I am able to destroy the temple of God, and, after three days, to rebuild it.' " (Matt 26:60-61)
Hail Mary...

The high priest, rising up, said to him, "Have you nothing to respond to what these ones testify against you?" But Jesus was silent. And the high priest said to him, "I bind you by an oath to the living God to tell us if you are the Christ, the Son of God." (Matt 26:62-63)
Hail Mary...

Jesus said to him: "You have said it. Yet truly I say to you, hereafter you shall see the Son of man sitting at the right hand of the power of God, and coming on the clouds of heaven." (Matt 26:64)
Hail Mary...

Then the high priest tore his garments, saying: "He has blasphemed. Why do we still need witnesses? Behold, you have now heard the blasphemy. How does it seem to you?" So they responded by saying, "He is guilty unto death."(Matt 26:65-66)
Hail Mary...

Then they spit in his face, and they struck him with fists. And others struck his face with the palms of their hands, saying: "Prophecy for us, O Christ. Who is the one that struck you?" (Matt 26:67-68)
Hail Mary...

Glory Be...

> *Christ above in torment hangs*
> *She beneath beholds the pangs*
> *Of her dying, glorious Son*

The Fourth Station

Jesus is Denied by Peter

Leader: We adore you, O Christ, and we bless you.

All: Because by your holy cross, you have redeemed the world.

Our Father...

Then Peter followed him from a distance, as far as the court of the high priest. And going inside, he sat down with the servants, so that he might see the end. (Matt 26:58)
Hail Mary...

Yet truly, Peter sat outside in the courtyard. And a maidservant approached him, saying, "You also were with Jesus the Galilean." But he denied it in the sight of them all, saying, "I do not know what you are saying." (Matt 26:69-70)
Hail Mary...

Then, as he exited by the gate, another maidservant saw him. And she said to those who were there, "This man also was with Jesus of Nazareth." (Matt 26:71)
Hail Mary...

And again, he denied it with an oath, "For I do not know the man." (Matt 26:72)
Hail Mary...

After a little while, those who were standing nearby came and said to Peter: "Truly, you also are one of them. For even your manner of speaking reveals you." (Matt 26:73)
Hail Mary...

Then he began to curse and to swear that he had not known the man. And immediately the rooster crowed. (Matt 26:74)
Hail Mary…

Peter remembered the words of Jesus, which he had said: "Before the rooster crows, you will deny me three times." And going outside, he wept bitterly. (Matt 26:75)
Hail Mary…

Glory Be…

> *Is there one who would not weep,*
> *'whelmed in miseries so deep*
> *Christ's dear Mother to behold.*

The Fifth Station

Jesus is Judged by Pilate

Leader: We adore you, O Christ, and we bless you.

All: Because by your holy cross, you have redeemed the world.

Our Father…

Immediately in the morning, after the leaders of the priests had taken counsel with the elders and the scribes and the entire council, binding Jesus, they led him away and delivered him to Pilate. (Mrk 15:1)
Hail Mary…

Pilate asked him. "Are you the king of the Jews?" But he answered, "You say so." (Mrk 15:2)
Hail Mary…

The leaders of the priests accused him in many things. Then Pilate again questioned him, saying: "Do you not have any response? See how greatly they accuse you." (Mrk 15:3-4)
Hail Mary…

But Jesus continued to give no response, so that Pilate wondered. Now on the feast day, he was accustomed to release to them one of the prisoners, whomever they requested. (Mrk 15:5-6)
Hail Mary…

Pilate answered them and said, "Do you want me to release to you the king of the Jews?" For he knew that it was out of envy that the leaders of the priests had betrayed him. (Mrk 15:9-10)
Hail Mary…

Then the chief priests incited the crowd, so that he would release Barabbas to them instead. But Pilate, responding again, said to them: "Then what do you want me to do with the king of the Jews?" But again they cried out, "Crucify him." (Mrk 15:11-13)
Hail Mary...

Yet truly, Pilate said to them: "Why? What evil has he done?" But they cried out all the more, "Crucify him." Then Pilate, wishing to satisfy the people, released Barabbas to them, and he delivered Jesus, having severely scourged him, to be crucified. (Mrk 15:14-15)
Hail Mary...

Glory Be...

> *Can the human heart refrain*
> *From partaking in her pain*
> *In that Mother's pain untold?*

The Sixth Station

Jesus is Scourged and Crowned with Thorns

Leader: We adore you, O Christ, and we bless you.

All: Because by your holy cross, you have redeemed the world.

Our Father...

Therefore, Pilate then took Jesus into custody and scourged him. (Jn 19:1)
Hail Mary...

Then the soldiers of the governor, taking Jesus up to the praetorium, gathered the entire cohort around him. (Matt 27:27)
Hail Mary...

Stripping him, they put a scarlet cloak around him. (Matt 27:28)
Hail Mary...

Plaiting a crown of thorns, they placed it on his head, with a reed in his right hand. And genuflecting before him, they mocked him, saying, "Hail, King of the Jews." (Matt 27:29)
Hail Mary...

Spitting on him, they took the reed and struck his head. (Matt 27:30)
Hail Mary...

Pilate went outside again, and he said to them: "Behold, I am bringing him out to you, so that you may realize that I find no case against him." So Jesus went out, bearing the crown of thorns and the purple garment. Pilate said to them, "Behold the man." (Jn 19:4-5)
Hail Mary...

After they had mocked him, they stripped him of the cloak, and clothed him with his own garments, and they led him away to crucify him. (Matt 27:31)
Hail Mary…

Glory Be…

> *Bruised, derided, cursed, defiled*
> *She beheld her tender Child*
> *All with bloody scourges rent.*

The Seventh Station

Jesus Bears the Cross

Leader: We adore you, O Christ, and we bless you.

All: Because by your holy cross, you have redeemed the world.

Our Father…

Therefore, when the high priests and the attendants had seen him, they cried out, saying: "Crucify him! Crucify him!" Pilate said to them: "Take him yourselves and crucify him. For I find no case against him." (Jn 19:6)
Hail Mary…

But they were crying out: "Take him away! Take him away! Crucify him!" Pilate said to them, "Shall I crucify your king?" The high priests responded, "We have no king except Caesar." (Jn 19:15)
Hail Mary…

Therefore, he then handed him over to them to be crucified. And they took Jesus and led him away. (Jn 19:16)
Hail Mary…

Carrying his own cross, he went forth to the place, which is called Calvary, but in Hebrew it is called the Place of the Skull. (Jn 19:17)
Hail Mary…

I have become a reproach among all my enemies, and especially my neighbors. Those who know me are afraid of me. When they see me, they flee from me. (Ps 31:11, Ps 30:12)
Hail Mary…

I have heard the blame of many, terror is all around me. While they assembled against me, they plot to take away my life. (Ps 31:13/ Ps 30:14)

Hail Mary…

Abraham took the wood of the burnt offering and laid it on his son Isaac, and he himself carried the fire and the knife. So the two of them walked on together. (Gen 22:6)

Hail Mary…

Glory Be…

> *For the sins of His own nation*
> *Saw Him hang in desolation*
> *Till His spirit forth He sent.*

The Eighth Station

Jesus is Helped by Simon the Cyrenian to Carry the Cross

Leader: We adore you, O Christ, and we bless you.

All: Because by your holy cross, you have redeemed the world.

Our Father...

As they were leading him away, they apprehended a certain one, Simon of Cyrene, as he was returning from the countryside. And they imposed the cross on him to carry after Jesus. (Luk 23:26)
Hail Mary...

They arrived at the place, which is called Golgotha, which is the place of Calvary. And they gave him wine to drink, mixed with gall. And when he had tasted it, he refused to drink it. (Matt 27:33-34)
Hail Mary...

I now rejoice in my sufferings for you, and in my flesh, complete those things that are lacking in the sufferings of Christ, for the sake of his body, which is the church. (Col 1:24)
Hail Mary...

Be glad, for these trials make you partake of the sufferings of Christ, so that you will have the wonderful joy of seeing his glory when it is revealed. (1 Pet 4:13)
Hail Mary...

Whoever does not bear his cross and come after me, is not able to be my disciple. (Luk 14:27)
Hail Mary...

I have been nailed to the cross with Christ. I live; yet now, it is not I, but truly Christ, who lives in me. Though I live now in the flesh, I live in the faith of the Son of God, who loved me and who delivered himself for me. (Gal 2:19-20)
Hail Mary…

If anyone is willing to come after me, let him deny himself, and take up his cross, and follow me. For whoever would save his life, will lose it. But whoever will have lost his life for my sake, shall find it. (Matt 16:24-25)
Hail Mary…

Glory Be…

O sweet Mother! Fount of Love,
Touch my spirit from above
Make my heart with yours accord

The Ninth Station

Jesus Meets the Women of Jerusalem

Leader: We adore you, O Christ, and we bless you.

All: Because by your holy cross, you have redeemed the world.

Our Father…

When he drew near, seeing the city, he wept over it, saying: "If only you had known, indeed even in this your day, which things are for your peace. But now they are hidden from your eyes. For the days will overtake you. And your enemies will encircle you with a valley. And they will surround you and hem you in on every side. (Luk 19:41-43)
Hail Mary…

Now there were also women watching from a distance, among whom were Mary Magdalene, and Mary the mother of James the younger and of Joseph, and Salome, (and while he was in Galilee, they followed him and ministered to him) and many other women, who had ascended along with him to Jerusalem. (Mrk 15:40-41)
Hail Mary…

Then a great crowd of people followed him, with women who were mourning and lamenting him. (Luk 23:27)
Hail Mary…

Jesus, turning to them, said: "Daughters of Jerusalem, do not weep over me. Instead, weep over yourselves and over your children." (Luk 23:28)
Hail Mary…

Behold, the days will arrive in which they will say, 'Blessed are the barren, and the wombs that have not borne, and the breasts that have not nursed.' (Luk 23:29)
Hail Mary…

Then they will begin to say to the mountains, 'Fall over us,' and to the hills, 'Cover us.' For if they do these things with green wood, what will be done with the dry?" (Luk 23:30-31)
Hail Mary…

Jerusalem, Jerusalem! You kill the prophets and stone those who have been sent to you. How often I have wanted to gather your children together, in the way that a hen gathers her young under her wings. But you were not willing! (Matt 23:37)
Hail Mary…

Glory Be…

> *Make me feel as You have felt*
> *Make my soul to glow and melt*
> *With the love of Christ, my Lord.*

The Tenth Station

Jesus is Crucified

Leader: We adore you, O Christ, and we bless you.
All: Because by your holy cross, you have redeemed the world.

Our Father...

When they arrived at the place that is called Calvary, they crucified him there, with the robbers, one to the right and the other to the left. (Luk 23:33)
Hail Mary...

Then Jesus said, "Father, forgive them. For they know not what they do." (Luk 23:34)
Hail Mary...

Then the soldiers, when they had crucified him, took his garments, and they made four parts, one part to each soldier, and the tunic. But the tunic was seamless, woven from above throughout the whole. Then they said to one another, "Let us not cut it, but instead let us cast lots over it, to see whose it will be." (Jn 19:23-24)
Hail Mary...

People were standing near, watching. And the leaders among them derided him, saying: "He saved others. Let him save himself, if this one is the Christ, the elect of God." (Luk 23:35)
Hail Mary...

The soldiers also ridiculed him, approaching him and offering him vinegar, and saying, "If you are the king of the Jews, save yourself." (Luk 23:36-37)
Hail Mary...

There was also an inscription written over him in letters of Greek, and Latin, and Hebrew: THIS IS THE KING OF THE JEWS. (Luk 23:38)
Hail Mary...

Let us gaze upon Jesus, as the Author and perfecter of our faith, who, having joy laid out before him, endured the cross, disregarding the shame, and who now sits at the right hand of the throne of God. (Heb 12:2)
Hail Mary...

Glory Be...

> *Holy Mother, pierce me through*
> *In my heart each wound renew*
> *Of my Savior crucified.*

The Eleventh Station

Leader: We adore you, O Christ, and we bless you.

All: Because by your holy cross, you have redeemed the world.

Our Father…

Two robbers were crucified with him: one on the right and one on the left. (Matt 27:38)
Hail Mary…

Those passing by blasphemed him, shaking their heads, and saying: "Ah, so you would destroy the temple of God and in three days rebuild it! Save your own self. If you are the Son of God, descend from the cross." (Matt 27:39-40)
Hail Mary…

And one of those robbers who were hanging blasphemed him, saying, "If you are the Christ, save yourself and us." (Luk 23:39)
Hail Mary…

But the other responded by rebuking him, saying: "Do you have no fear of God, since you are under the same condemnation? (Luk 23:40)
Hail Mary…

Indeed, it is just for us. For we are receiving what our deeds deserve. But truly, this man has done nothing wrong." (Luk 23:41)
Hail Mary…

He said to Jesus, "Lord, remember me when you come into your kingdom." (Luk 23:42)

Hail Mary…

Jesus said to him, "Amen I say to you, this day you shall be with me in Paradise." (Luk 23:43)
Hail Mary…

Glory Be…

> *Let me share with you His pain,*
> *Who for all our sins was slain,*
> *Who for me in torments died.*

The Twelfth Station

Jesus Speaks to His Mother and the Disciple

Leader: We adore you, O Christ, and we bless you.

All: Because by your holy cross, you have redeemed the world.

Our Father...

Standing beside the cross of Jesus were his mother, and his mother's sister, and Mary of Cleophas, and Mary Magdalene. (Jn 19:25)
Hail Mary...

Therefore, when Jesus had seen his mother and the disciple whom he loved standing near, he said to his mother, "Woman, behold your son." (Jn 19:26)
Hail Mary...

Next, he said to the disciple, "Behold your mother." (Jn 19:27)
Hail Mary...

From that hour, the disciple accepted her as his own. (Jn 19:27)
Hail Mary...

After this, Jesus knew that all had been accomplished, so in order that the Scripture might be completed, he said, "I thirst." (Jn 19:28)
Hail Mary...

There was a container placed there, full of vinegar. Then, placing a sponge full of vinegar around hyssop, they brought it to his mouth. Then Jesus, when he had received the vinegar, said: "It is finished." And bowing down his head, he gave up his spirit. (Jn 19:29-30)
Hail Mary...

Then the Jews, because it was the preparation day, so that the bodies would not remain upon the cross on the Sabbath, they petitioned Pilate in order that their legs might be broken, and they might be taken away. (Jn 19:31)
Hail Mary…

Glory Be…

> *Let me mingle tears with thee*
> *Mourning Him who mourned for me,*
> *All the days that I may live.*

The Thirteenth Station

Jesus Dies on the Cross

Leader: We adore you, O Christ, and we bless you.

All: Because by your holy cross, you have redeemed the world.

Our Father...

It was nearly the sixth hour, and a darkness occurred over the entire earth, until the ninth hour. (Luk 23:44)
Hail Mary...

The sun was obscured; and the veil of the temple was torn down the middle. (Luk 23:45)
Hail Mary...

Jesus, crying out with a loud voice, said: "Father, into your hands I commend my spirit." And upon saying this, he breathed his last. (Luk 23:46)
Hail Mary...

The centurion, seeing what had happened, glorified God, saying, "Truly, this man was innocent." (Luk 23:47)
Hail Mary...

The entire crowd of those who came together to see this spectacle also saw what had happened, and they returned, striking their breasts. (Luk 23:48)
Hail Mary...

Now all those who knew him, and the women who had followed him from Galilee, were standing at a distance, watching these things. (Luk 23:49)
Hail Mary...

For this reason, the Father loves me: because I lay down my life, so that I may take it up again. No one takes it away from me. Instead, I lay it down of my own accord. And I have the power to lay it down. And I have the power to take it up again. This is the commandment that I have received from my Father. (Jn 10:17-18)
Hail Mary...

Glory Be...

> *By the cross with you to stay*
> *There with you to weep and pray*
> *Is all I ask of you to give.*

The Fourteenth Station

Jesus is Placed in the Tomb

Leader: We adore you, O Christ, and we bless you.

All: Because by your holy cross, you have redeemed the world.

Our Father...

Behold, there was a man named Joseph, who was a councilman, a good and just man, (for he had not consented to their decision or their actions). He was from Arimathea, a city of Judea. And he was himself also anticipating the kingdom of God. (Luk 23:50-51)
Hail Mary...

This man approached Pilate and petitioned for the body of Jesus. (Luk 23:52)
Hail Mary...

Now Nicodemus also arrived, (who had gone to Jesus at first by night) bringing a mixture of myrrh and aloe, weighing about seventy pounds. (Jn 19:39)
Hail Mary...

Taking him down, he wrapped him in a fine linen cloth, and he placed him in a tomb hewn from rock, in which no one had ever been placed. (Luk 23:53)
Hail Mary...

It was the day of Preparation, and the Sabbath was drawing near. (Luk 23:54)
Hail Mary...

Now the women who had come with him from Galilee, by following, saw the tomb and the manner in which his body was placed. (Luk 23:55)
Hail Mary…

Upon returning, they prepared aromatic spices and ointments. But on the Sabbath, indeed, they rested, according to the commandment. (Luk 23:56)
Hail Mary…

Glory Be…

Virgin of all virgins blest!
Listen to my fond request:
Let me share your grief divine.

Closing Prayer

(All): Behold, O kind and most sweet Jesus, I cast myself upon my knees in Your sight, and with the most fervent desire of my soul, I pray and beseech You that You would impress upon my heart lively sentiments of Faith, Hope and Charity, with true contrition for my sins and a firm purpose of amendment; while with deep affection and grief of soul, I ponder within myself and mentally contemplate Your five wounds, having before my eyes the words which David the prophet put on Your lips concerning You: "They have pierced My hands and My feet, they have numbered all My bones." Amen

For the intentions of the Holy Father

Our Father…

Hail Mary…

Glory Be…Amen

Scriptural Stations of the Cross
(Shorter Version)

*Based on the stations celebrated by Pope John
Paul II on Good Friday 1991*

Opening Prayer

Leader: My Lord, Jesus Christ, You have made this journey to die for me with unspeakable love; and I have so many times ungratefully abandoned You. But now I love You with all my heart; and, because I love You, I am sincerely sorry for ever having offended You. Pardon me, my God, and permit me to accompany You on this journey. You go to die for love of me; I want, my beloved Redeemer, to die for love of You. My Jesus, I will live and die always united to You.

*At the cross her station keeping
Stood the mournful Mother weeping
Close to Jesus to the last*

The First Station

Jesus in the Garden of Gethsemane

Leader: We adore you, O Christ, and we bless you.

All: Because by your holy cross, you have redeemed the world.

Jesus went with them to a garden, which is called Gethsemane; and he said to his disciples, "Sit down here, while I go there and pray." Taking with him Peter and the two sons of Zebedee, he began to be sorrowful and saddened. Then he said to them: "My soul is sorrowful, even unto death. Stay here and keep vigil with me." Continuing on a little further, he fell prostrate on his face, praying and saying: "My Father, if it is possible, let this chalice pass away from me. Yet truly, let it not be as I will, but as you will." He approached his disciples and found them sleeping. And he said to Peter: "So, were you not able to keep vigil with me for one hour? Be vigilant and pray, so that you may not enter into temptation. Indeed, the spirit is willing, but the flesh is weak." (Matt 26:37-41)

Our Father…

Hail Mary…

Glory Be…

Through her heart, His sorrow sharing
All His bitter anguish bearing
Now at length the sword has passed

The Second Station

Jesus, Betrayed by Judas, is Arrested

Leader: We adore you, O Christ, and we bless you.

All: Because by your holy cross, you have redeemed the world.

While he was still speaking, behold, Judas, one of the twelve, arrived, and with him was a large crowd with swords and clubs, sent from the leaders of the priests and the elders of the people. He who betrayed him gave them a sign, saying: "Whomever I will kiss, it is he. Take hold of him." And quickly drawing close to Jesus, he said, "Hail, Master." And he kissed him. Jesus said to him, "Friend, for what purpose have you come?" Then they approached, and they put their hands on Jesus, and they arrested him. (Matt 26:47-50)

Our Father…

Hail Mary…

Glory Be…

> *O, how sad and sore depressed*
> *Was that Mother highly blessed*
> *Of the sole Begotten One*

The Third Station

Jesus is Condemned by the Sanhedrin

Leader: We adore you, O Christ, and we bless you.

All: Because by your holy cross, you have redeemed the world.

When it was daytime, the elders of the people, and the leaders of the priests, and the scribes convened. And they led him into their council, saying, "If you are the Christ, tell us." And he said to them: "If I tell you, you will not believe me. And if I also question you, you will not answer me. Neither will you release me. But from this time, the Son of man will be sitting at the right hand of the power of God." Then they all said, "So you are the Son of God?" And he said. "You are saying that I am." And they said: "Why do we still require testimony? For we have heard it ourselves, from his own mouth." (Luk 22:66-71)

Our Father…

Hail Mary…

Glory Be…

Christ above in torment hangs
She beneath beholds the pangs
Of her dying, glorious Son

The Fourth Station

Leader: We adore you, O Christ, and we bless you.

All: Because by your holy cross, you have redeemed the world.

Yet truly, Peter sat outside in the courtyard. And a maidservant approached him, saying, "You also were with Jesus the Galilean." But he denied it in the sight of them all, saying, "I do not know what you are saying." Then, as he exited by the gate, another maidservant saw him. And she said to those who were there, "This man also was with Jesus of Nazareth." And again, he denied it with an oath, "For I do not know the man." After a little while, those who were standing nearby came and said to Peter: "Truly, you also are one of them. For even your manner of speaking reveals you." Then he began to curse and to swear that he had not known the man. And immediately the rooster crowed. Peter remembered the words of Jesus, which he had said: "Before the rooster crows, you will deny me three times." And going outside, he wept bitterly. (Matt 26:69-75)

Our Father…

Hail Mary…

Glory Be…

> *Is there one who would not weep,*
> *'whelmed in miseries so deep*
> *Christ's dear Mother to behold*

The Fifth Station

Jesus is Judged by Pilate

Leader: We adore you, O Christ, and we bless you.
All: Because by your holy cross, you have redeemed the world.

After the leaders of the priests had taken counsel with the elders and the scribes and the entire council, binding Jesus, they led him away and delivered him to Pilate. Pilate asked him, "Are you the King of the Jews?" He answered him, "You say so." The leaders of the priests accused him in many things. Then Pilate again questioned him, saying: "Do you not have any response? See how greatly they accuse you." But Jesus continued to give no response, so that Pilate wondered. Now on the feast day, he was accustomed to release to them one of the prisoners, whomever they requested. Pilate answered them and said, "Do you want me to release to you the king of the Jews?" For he knew that it was out of envy that the leaders of the priests had betrayed him. The chief priests incited the crowd, so that he would release Barabbas to them instead. But Pilate, responding again, said to them: "Then what do you want me to do with the king of the Jews?" But again they cried out, "Crucify him." Yet truly, Pilate said to them: "Why? What evil has he done?" But they cried out all the more, "Crucify him." Then Pilate, wishing to satisfy the people, released Barabbas to them, and he delivered Jesus, having severely scourged him, to be crucified. (Mrk 15:1-6, 9-15)

Our Father.... Hail Mary.... Glory Be....

Can the human heart refrain
From partaking in her pain
In that Mother's pain untold?

The Sixth Station

Jesus is Scourged and Crowned with Thorns

Leader: We adore you, O Christ, and we bless you.

All: Because by your holy cross, you have redeemed the world.

Therefore, Pilate then took Jesus into custody and scourged him. And the soldiers, plaiting a crown of thorns, imposed it on his head. And they put a purple garment around him. And they were approaching him and saying, "Hail, king of the Jews!" And they struck him repeatedly. Pilate went outside again, and he said to them: "Behold, I am bringing him out to you, so that you may realize that I find no case against him." So Jesus went out, bearing the crown of thorns and the purple garment. Pilate said to them, "Behold the man." (Jn 19:1-5)

Our Father…

Hail Mary…

Glory Be…

> *Bruised, derided, cursed, defiled*
> *She beheld her tender Child*
> *All with bloody scourges rent*

The Seventh Station

Jesus Bears the Cross

Leader: We adore you, O Christ, and we bless you.
All: Because by your holy cross, you have redeemed the world.

Therefore, when the high priests and the attendants had seen him, they cried out, saying: "Crucify him! Crucify him!" Pilate said to them: "Take him yourselves and crucify him. For I find no case against him."… But they were crying out: "Take him away! Take him away! Crucify him!" Pilate said to them, "Shall I crucify your king?" The high priests responded, "We have no king except Caesar." Therefore, he then handed him over to them to be crucified. And they took Jesus and led him away. Carrying his own cross, he went forth to the place, which is called Calvary, but in Hebrew it is called the Place of the Skull. (Jn 19:6, 15-17)

Our Father…

Hail Mary…

Glory Be…

> *For the sins of His own nation*
> *Saw Him hang in desolation*
> *Till His spirit forth He sent*

The Eighth Station

Jesus is Helped by Simon the Cyrenian to Carry the Cross

Leader: We adore you, O Christ, and we bless you.

All: Because by your holy cross, you have redeemed the world.

As they were going out, they came upon a man of Cyrene, named Simon, whom they compelled to take up his cross. They arrived at the place which is called Golgotha, which is the place of Calvary. And they gave him wine to drink, mixed with gall. And when he had tasted it, he refused to drink it. (Matt 27:32-34)

Our Father...

Hail Mary...

Glory Be...

> *O sweet Mother! Fount of Love,*
> *Touch my spirit from above*
> *Make my heart with yours accord*

The Ninth Station

Jesus Meets the Women of Jerusalem

Leader: We adore you, O Christ, and we bless you.

All: Because by your holy cross, you have redeemed the world.

Then a great crowd of people followed him, with women who were mourning and lamenting him. Jesus, turning to them, said: "Daughters of Jerusalem, do not weep over me. Instead, weep over yourselves and over your children." Behold, the days will arrive in which they will say, 'Blessed are the barren, and the wombs that have not borne, and the breasts that have not nursed.' Then they will begin to say to the mountains, 'Fall over us,' and to the hills, 'Cover us.' For if they do these things with green wood, what will be done with the dry?" (Luk 23:27-31)

Our Father…

Hail Mary…

Glory Be…

> *Make me feel as You have felt*
> *Make my soul to glow and melt*
> *With the love of Christ, my Lord*

The Tenth Station

Jesus is Crucified

Leader: We adore you, O Christ, and we bless you.

All: Because by your holy cross, you have redeemed the world.

When they arrived at the place that is called Calvary, they crucified him there, with the robbers, one to the right and the other to the left. Then Jesus said, "Father, forgive them. For they know not what they do."People were standing near, watching. And the leaders among them derided him, saying: "He saved others. Let him save himself, if this one is the Christ, the elect of God." The soldiers also ridiculed him, approaching him and offering him vinegar, and saying, "If you are the king of the Jews, save yourself." There was also an inscription written over him in letters of Greek, and Latin, and Hebrew: THIS IS THE KING OF THE JEWS. (Luk 23:33-38)

Our Father...

Hail Mary...

Glory Be...

> *Holy Mother, pierce me through*
> *In my heart each wound renew*
> *Of my Savior crucified*

The Eleventh Station

*Jesus Promises His Kingdom to the Good
Thief*

One of those robbers who were hanging blasphemed him, saying, "If you are the Christ, save yourself and us." But the other responded by rebuking him, saying: "Do you have no fear of God, since you are under the same condemnation? Indeed, it is just for us. For we are receiving what our deeds deserve. But truly, this man has done nothing wrong." He said to Jesus, "Lord, remember me when you come into your kingdom." Jesus said to him, "Amen I say to you, this day you shall be with me in Paradise." (Luk 23:39-43)

Our Father…

Hail Mary…

Glory Be…

> *Let me share with you His pain,*
> *Who for all our sins was slain,*
> *Who for me in torments died*

45

The Twelfth Station

Jesus Speaks to His Mother and the Disciple

Leader: We adore you, O Christ, and we bless you.

All: Because by your holy cross, you have redeemed the world.

Standing beside the cross of Jesus were his mother, and his mother's sister, and Mary of Cleophas, and Mary Magdalene. Therefore, when Jesus had seen his mother and the disciple whom he loved standing near, he said to his mother, "Woman, behold your son." Next, he said to the disciple, "Behold your mother." From that hour, the disciple accepted her as his own. (Jn 19:25-27)

Our Father…

Hail Mary…

Glory Be…

> *Let me mingle tears with thee*
> *Mourning Him who mourned for me,*
> *All the days that I may live*

The Thirteenth Station

Jesus Dies on the Cross

It was nearly the sixth hour, and a darkness occurred over the entire earth, until the ninth hour. The sun was obscured; and the veil of the temple was torn down the middle. Jesus, crying out with a loud voice, said: "Father, into your hands I commend my spirit." And upon saying this, he breathed his last. The centurion, seeing what had happened, glorified God, saying, "Truly, this man was innocent." The entire crowd of those who came together to see this spectacle also saw what had happened, and they returned, striking their breasts. (Luk 23:44-48)

Our Father…

Hail Mary…

Glory Be…

> *By the cross with you to stay*
> *There with you to weep and pray*
> *Is all I ask of you to give*

The Fourteenth Station

Jesus is Placed in the Tomb

Leader: We adore you, O Christ, and we bless you.

All: Because by your holy cross, you have redeemed the world.

Behold, there was a man named Joseph, who was a councilman, a good and just man, (for he had not consented to their decision or their actions). He was from Arimathea, a city of Judea. And he was himself also anticipating the kingdom of God. This man approached Pilate and petitioned for the body of Jesus. Taking him down, he wrapped him in a fine linen cloth, and he placed him in a tomb hewn from rock, in which no one had ever been placed. (Luk 23:50-53)

Our Father...

Hail Mary...

Glory Be...

Virgin of all virgins blest!
Listen to my fond request:
Let me share your grief divine

Closing Prayer

(All): Behold, O kind and most sweet Jesus, I cast myself upon my knees in Your sight, and with the most fervent desire of my soul, I pray and beseech You that You would impress upon my heart lively sentiments of Faith, Hope and Charity, with true contrition for my sins and a firm purpose of amendment; while with deep affection and grief of soul, I ponder within myself and mentally contemplate Your five wounds, having before my eyes the words which David the prophet put on Your lips concerning You: "They have pierced My hands and My feet, they have numbered all My bones." Amen

For the intentions of the Holy Father

Our Father…

Hail Mary…

Glory Be…

Amen.

The Traditional Stations of the Cross

As composed by Saint Alphonsus Ligouri

Opening Prayer:

Leader: My Lord, Jesus Christ, You have made this journey to die for me with unspeakable love; and I have so many times ungratefully abandoned You. But now I love You with all my heart; and, because I love You, I am sincerely sorry for ever having offended You. Pardon me, my God, and permit me to accompany You on this journey. You go to die for love of me; I want, my beloved Redeemer, to die for love of You. My Jesus, I will live and die always united to You.

At the cross her station keeping
Stood the mournful Mother weeping
Close to Jesus to the last

The First Station

Jesus is condemned to death

Leader: We adore you, O Christ, and we bless you.
All: Because by your holy cross, you have redeemed the world.

Leader: Consider how Jesus, after having been scourged and crowned with thorns, was unjustly condemned by Pilate to die on the Cross.

All: My adorable Jesus, it was not Pilate, no, it was my sins that condemned You to die. I beseech You, by the merits of this sorrowful journey, to assist my soul in its journey towards eternity. I love You, my beloved Jesus; I repent with my whole heart for having offended You. Never permit me to separate myself from You again. Grant that I may love You always; and then do with me what You will.

Our Father…

Hail Mary…

Glory Be…

Through her heart, His sorrow sharing
All His bitter anguish bearing
Now at length the sword has passed

The Second Station

Jesus carries His cross

Leader: We adore you, O Christ, and we bless you.
All: Because by your holy cross, you have redeemed the world.

Leader: Consider how Jesus, in making this journey with the cross on His shoulders thought of us, and for us offered to His Father the death He was about to undergo.

All: My most beloved Jesus, I embrace all the tribulations You have destined for me until death. I beseech You, by the merits of the pain You did suffer in carrying Your Cross, to give me the necessary help to carry mine with perfect patience and resignation. I love You, Jesus my love; I repent for having offended You. Never permit me to separate myself from You again. Grant that I may love You always; and then do with me what You will.

Our Father…

Hail Mary…

Glory Be…

O, how sad and sore depressed
Was that Mother highly blessed
Of the sole Begotten One

The Third Station

Jesus falls the first time

Leader: We adore you, O Christ, and we bless you.
All: Because by your holy cross, you have redeemed the world.

Leader: Consider this first fall of Jesus under His Cross. His flesh was torn by the scourges; His head crowned with thorns, and He had lost a great quantity of blood. He was so weakened that He could scarcely walk, and yet He had to carry this great load upon His shoulders. The soldiers struck Him rudely, and thus He fell several times in His journey.

All: My most beloved Jesus, it is not the weight of the Cross, but my sins, which have made You suffer so much pain. Ah, by the merits of this first fall, deliver me from the misfortune of falling into mortal sin. I love You, O my Jesus, with my whole heart; I repent for having offended You. Never permit me to separate myself from You again. Grant that I may love You always; and then do with me what You will.

Our Father…

Hail Mary…

Glory Be…

> *Christ above in torment hangs*
> *She beneath beholds the pangs*
> *Of her dying, glorious Son*

The Fourth Station

Jesus meets his mother

Leader: We adore you, O Christ, and we bless you.
All: Because by your holy cross, you have redeemed the world.

Leader: Consider how the Son met his Mother on His way to Calvary. Jesus and Mary gazed at each other and their looks became as so many arrows to wound those hearts which loved each other so tenderly

All: My most loving Jesus, by the pain You suffered in this meeting, grant me the grace of being truly devoted to Your most holy Mother. And You, my Queen, who was overwhelmed with sorrow, obtain for me by Your prayers a tender and a lasting remembrance of the passion of Your divine Son. I love You, Jesus, my Love, above all things. I repent of ever having offended You. Never allow me to offend You again. Grant that I may love You always; and then do with me as You will.

Our Father…

Hail Mary…

Glory Be…

> *Is there one who would not weep,*
> *'whelmed in miseries so deep*
> *Christ's dear Mother to behold.*

The Fifth Station

Leader: We adore you, O Christ, and we bless you.
All: Because by your holy cross, you have redeemed the world.

Leader: Consider how the Jews, seeing that each step Jesus took was weakening Him to the point of expiring, and fearing that He would die on the way, when they wished Him to die the ignominious death of the Cross, constrained Simon the Cyrenian to carry the Cross behind our Lord.

All: My most sweet Jesus, I will not refuse the Cross, as the Cyrenian did; I accept it; I embrace it. I accept in particular the death You have destined for me; with all the pains that may accompany it; I unite it to Your death; I offer it to You. You have died for love of me; I will die for love of You, and to please You. Help me by Your grace. I love You, Jesus my love; I repent for having offended You. Never permit me to offend You again. Grant that I may love You always; and then do with me what You will.

Our Father…

Hail Mary…

Glory Be…

> *Can the human heart refrain*
> *From partaking in her pain*
> *In that Mother's pain untold?*

The Sixth Station

Veronica wipes the face of Jesus

Leader: We adore you, O Christ, and we bless you.
All: Because by your holy cross, you have redeemed the world.

Leader: Consider how the holy woman named Veronica, seeing Jesus so afflicted, and His face bathed in sweat and blood, presented Him with a towel, with which He wiped His adorable face, leaving on it the impression of His holy countenance.

All: My most beloved Jesus, your face was beautiful before, but in this journey, it has lost all its beauty, and wounds and blood have disfigured it. Alas, my soul also was once beautiful, when it received Your grace in Baptism, but I have disfigured it since by my sins. You alone, my Redeemer, can restore it to its former beauty. Do this by Your Passion, O Jesus. I repent for having offended You. Never permit me to offend You again. Grant that I may love You always; and then do with me what You will.

Our Father…

Hail Mary…

Glory Be…

Bruised, derided, cursed, defiled
She beheld her tender Child
All with bloody scourges rent.

The Seventh Station

Jesus falls the second time

Leader: We adore you, O Christ, and we bless you.
All: Because by your holy cross, you have redeemed the world.

Leader: Consider the second fall of Jesus under the Cross, a fall which renews the pain of all the wounds of the head and members of our afflicted Lord.

All: My most gentle Jesus, how many times You have pardoned me, and how many times have I fallen again, and begun again to offend You. Oh, by the merits of this new fall, give me the necessary help to persevere in Your grace until death. Grant that in all temptations which assail me I may always commend myself to You. I love You, Jesus my love; I repent for having offended You. Never permit me to offend You again. Grant that I may love You always; and then do with me what You will.

Our Father…

Hail Mary…

Glory Be…

> *For the sins of His own nation*
> *Saw Him hang in desolation*
> *Till His spirit forth He sent.*

The Eighth Station

Jesus meets the women of Jerusalem

Leader: We adore you, O Christ, and we bless you.
All: Because by your holy cross, you have redeemed the world.

Leader: Consider how those women wept with compassion at seeing Jesus in such a pitiable state, streaming with blood, as He walked along. But Jesus said to them: "Weep not for Me, but for your children".

All: My Jesus, laden with sorrows, I weep for the offenses I have committed against You, because of the pains they have deserved, and still more because of the displeasure they have caused You, who have loved me so much. It is Your love, more than the fear of hell, which causes me to weep for my sins. My Jesus, I love You more than myself; I repent for having offended You. Never permit me to offend You again. Grant that I may love You always; and then do with me what You will.

Our Father…

Hail Mary…

Glory Be…

O sweet Mother! Fount of Love,
Touch my spirit from above
Make my heart with yours accord.

The Ninth Station

Jesus falls a third time

Leader: We adore you, O Christ, and we bless you.
All: Because by your holy cross, you have redeemed the world.

Leader: Consider the third fall of Jesus Christ. His weakness was extreme, and the cruelty of His executioners was excessive, who tried to hasten His steps when He had scarcely strength to move.

All: Ah, my outraged Jesus, by the merits of the weakness You did suffer in going to Calvary, give me strength sufficient to conquer all human respect, and all my wicked passions, which have led me to despise Your friendship. I love You, Jesus my love, with my whole heart; I repent for having offended You. Never permit me to offend You again. Grant that I may love You always; and then do with me what You will.

Our Father…

Hail Mary…

Glory Be…

> *Make me feel as You have felt*
> *Make my soul to glow and melt*
> *With the love of Christ, my Lord.*

The Tenth Station

Jesus is Stripped of his garments

Leader: We adore you, O Christ, and we bless you.
All: Because by your holy cross, you have redeemed the world.

Leader: Consider the violence with which the executioners stripped Jesus. His inner garments adhered to His torn flesh, and they dragged them off so roughly that the skin came with them. Comfort your Savior that was cruelly treated, and say to Him:

All: My innocent Jesus, by the merits of the torment You felt, help me to strip myself of all affection to things of earth, in order that I may place all my love in You, who are so worthy of my love. I love You, O Jesus, with my whole heart; I repent for having offended You. Never permit me to offend You again. Grant that I may love You always; and then do with me what You will.

Our Father...

Hail Mary...

Glory Be...

Holy Mother, pierce me through
In my heart each wound renew
Of my Savior crucified.

The Eleventh Station

Jesus is nailed to the cross

Leader: We adore you, O Christ, and we bless you.
All: Because by your holy cross, you have redeemed the world.

Leader: Consider how Jesus, after being thrown on the Cross, extended His hands and offered to His Eternal Father the sacrifice of His death for our salvation. These barbarians fastened Him with nails, and then, raising the Cross, allowed Him to die with anguish on this infamous gibbet.

All: My Jesus! Loaded with contempt, nail my heart to Your feet, that it may ever remain there, to love You, and never quit You again. I love You more than myself; I repent for having offended You. Never permit me to offend You again. Grant that I may love You always; and then do with me what You will.

Our Father...

Hail Mary...

Glory Be...

Let me share with you His pain,
Who for all our sins was slain,
Who for me in torments died.

The Twelfth Station

Jesus dies on the cross

Leader: We adore you, O Christ, and we bless you.
All: Because by your holy cross, you have redeemed the world.

Leader: Consider how Jesus, after three hours of Agony on the Cross, consumed at length with anguish, abandons Himself to the weight of His body, bows His head, and dies.

All: O my dying Jesus, I kiss devoutly the Cross on which You died for love of me. I have merited by my sins to die a miserable death; but Your death is my hope. Ah, by the merits of Your death, give me the grace to die, embracing Your feet, and burning with love for You. I yield my soul into Your hands. I love You with my whole heart; I repent for ever having offended You. Never permit me to offend You again. Grant that I may love You always; and then do with me what You will.

Our Father...

Hail Mary...

Glory Be...

> *Let me mingle tears with thee*
> *Mourning Him who mourned for me,*
> *All the days that I may live.*

The Thirteenth Station

The body of Jesus is taken down from the cross

Leader: We adore you, O Christ, and we bless you.
All: Because by your holy cross, you have redeemed the world.

Leader: Consider how, after the death of our Lord, two of His disciples, Joseph and Nicodemus, took Him down from the cross, and placed Him in the arms of His afflicted Mother, who received Him with unutterable tenderness, and pressed Him to her bosom.

All: O Mother of sorrow, for the love of your Son, accept me as your servant, and pray to Him for me. And You, my Redeemer, since You have died for me, permit me to love You; for I wish for You, and nothing more. I love You, my Jesus, and I repent for ever having offended You. Never permit me to offend You again. Grant that I may love You always; and then do with me what You will.

Our Father…

Hail Mary…

Glory Be…

By the cross with you to stay
There with you to weep and pray
Is all I ask of you to give.

The Fourteenth Station

Jesus is laid in the tomb

Leader: We adore you, O Christ, and we bless you.
All: Because by your holy cross, you have redeemed the world.

Leader: Consider how the disciples carried the body of Jesus to bury it, accompanied by His holy Mother, who arranged it in the sepulchre with her own hands. They then closed the tomb, and all withdrew.

All: Oh, my buried Jesus, I kiss the stone that enclosed You. But You rose again on the third day. I beseech You, by Your resurrection, make me rise gloriously with You on the last day, to be always united with You in heaven, to praise You and love You forever. I love You, and I repent for ever having offended You. Never permit me to offend You again. Grant that I may love You always; and then do with me what You will.

Our Father...

Hail Mary...

Glory Be:

Virgin of all virgins blest!
Listen to my fond request:
Let me share your grief divine.

Closing Prayer

Prayer to Jesus crucified

Behold, O kind and most sweet Jesus, I cast myself upon my knees in Your sight, and with the most fervent desire of my soul, I pray and beseech You that You would impress upon my heart lively sentiments of Faith, Hope and Charity, with true contrition for my sins and a firm purpose of amendment; while with deep affection and grief of soul, I ponder within myself and mentally contemplate Your five wounds, having before my eyes the words which David the prophet put on Your lips concerning You: "They have pierced My hands and My feet, they have numbered all My bones."

For the intentions of the Holy Father

Our Father…

Hail Mary…

Glory Be…

Amen

Passion Rosary I

According to the Gospel of St. Matthew
(Synoptic Gospels)

Decade 1

Our Father...

While he was still speaking, behold, Judas, one of the twelve, arrived, and with him was a large crowd with swords and clubs, sent from the leaders of the priests and the elders of the people. (Matt 26:47)
Hail Mary...

He who betrayed him gave them a sign, saying: "Whomever I will kiss, it is he. Take hold of him." And quickly drawing close to Jesus, he said, "Hail, Master." And he kissed him. (Matt 26:48-49)
Hail Mary...

Jesus said to him, "Friend, for what purpose have you come?" Then they approached, and they put their hands on Jesus, and they arrested him. (Matt 26:50)
Hail Mary...

Behold, one of those who were with Jesus, extending his hand, drew his sword and struck the servant of the high priest, cutting off his ear. (Matt 26:51)
Hail Mary...

Then Jesus said to him: "Put your sword back in its place. For all who take up the sword shall perish by the sword. (Matt 26:52)
Hail Mary...

Do you think that I cannot ask my Father, so that he would give me, even now, more than twelve legions of Angels? How then would the Scriptures be fulfilled, which say that it must be so?" (Matt 26:53-54)

Hail Mary…

In that same hour, Jesus said to the crowds: "You went out, as if to a robber, with swords and clubs to seize me. Yet I sat daily with you, teaching in the temple, and you did not take hold of me. (Matt 26:55)

Hail Mary…

But all this has happened so that the Scriptures of the prophets may be fulfilled." Then all the disciples fled, abandoning him. (Matt 26:56)

Hail Mary…

Those who were holding Jesus led him to Caiaphas, the high priest, where the scribes and the elders had joined together. (Matt 26:57)

Hail Mary…

Then Peter followed him from a distance, as far as the court of the high priest. And going inside, he sat down with the servants, so that he might see the end. (Matt 26:58)

Hail Mary…

Glory Be…

Decade 2

Our Father…

Then the leaders of the priests and the entire council sought false testimony against Jesus, so that they might deliver him to death. (Matt 26:59)

Hail Mary…

And they did not find any, even though many false witnesses had come forward. Then, at the very end, two false witnesses came forward, and they said, "This man said: 'I am able to destroy the

temple of God, and, after three days, to rebuild it.' " (Matt 26:60-61)
Hail Mary…

And the high priest, rising up, said to him, "Have you nothing to respond to what these ones testify against you?" (Matt 26:62)
Hail Mary…

But Jesus was silent. And the high priest said to him, "I bind you by an oath to the living God to tell us if you are the Christ, the Son of God." (Matt 26:63)
Hail Mary…

Jesus said to him: "You have said it. Yet truly I say to you, hereafter you shall see the Son of man sitting at the right hand of the power of God, and coming on the clouds of heaven." (Matt 26:64)
Hail Mary…

Then the high priest tore his garments, saying: "He has blasphemed. Why do we still need witnesses? Behold, you have now heard the blasphemy. So they responded by saying, "He is guilty unto death." (Matt 26:65-66)
Hail Mary…

Then they spit in his face, and they struck him with fists. And others struck his face with the palms of their hands, saying: "Prophesy for us, O Christ. Who is the one that struck you?" (Matt 26:67-68)
Hail Mary…

When morning arrived, all the leaders of the priests and the elders of the people took counsel against Jesus, so that they might deliver him to death. (Matt 27:1)
Hail Mary…

And they led him, bound, and handed him over to Pontius Pilate, the governor. (Matt 27:2)
Hail Mary…

Then Judas, who betrayed him, seeing that he had been condemned, regretting his conduct, brought back the thirty pieces of silver to the leaders of the priests and the elders, saying, "I have sinned in betraying just blood." But they said to him: "What is that to us? See to it yourself." (Matt 27:3-4)
Hail Mary…

Glory Be…

Decade 3

Our Father…

Throwing down the pieces of silver in the temple, he departed. And going out, he hanged himself with a snare. But the leaders of the priests, having taken up the pieces of silver, said, "It is not lawful to put them into the temple offerings, because it is the price of blood." (Matt 27:5-6)
Hail Mary…

Now Jesus stood before the governor, and the governor questioned him, saying, "You are the king of the Jews?" Jesus said to him, "You are saying so." (Matt 27:11)
Hail Mary…

When he was accused by the leaders of the priests and the elders, he responded nothing. (Matt 27:12)
Hail Mary…

Then Pilate said to him, "Do you not hear how much testimony they speak against you?" And he did not respond any word to him, so that the governor wondered greatly. (Matt 27:13-14)
Hail Mary…

Pilate said to them, "Who is it that you want me to release to you: Barabbas, or Jesus, who is called Christ?" For he knew that it was out of envy they had handed him over. (Matt 27:17-18)
Hail Mary…

As he was sitting in the place of judgment, his wife sent to him, saying: Have you nothing to do with that just man; for I have suffered many things because of a dream about him. (Matt 27:19)
Hail Mary...

The leaders of the priests and the elders persuaded the people, so that they would ask for Barabbas, and so that Jesus would be killed. Then, in response, the governor said to them, "Which of the two do you want to be released to you?" But they said to him, "Barabbas." (Matt 27:20-21)
Hail Mary...

Pilate said to them, "Then what shall I do about Jesus, who is called Christ?" They all said, "Let him be crucified." The governor said to them, "But what evil has he done?" But they cried out all the more, saying, "Let him be crucified." (Matt 27:22-23)
Hail Mary...

Then Pilate, seeing that he was able to accomplish nothing, but that a greater tumult was occurring, taking water, washed his hands in the sight of the people, saying: "I am innocent of the blood of this just man. See to it yourselves." (Matt 27:24)
Hail Mary...

The entire people responded by saying, "May his blood be upon us and upon our children." Then he released Barabbas to them. But Jesus, having been scourged, he handed over to them, so that he would be crucified. (Matt 27:25-26)
Hail Mary...

Glory Be...

Decade 4

Our Father...

Then the soldiers of the governor, taking Jesus up to the governor's headquarters, gathered the entire cohort around him. And stripping him, they put a scarlet cloak around him. (Matt 27:27-28)

Hail Mary…

Twisting some thorns into a crown, they placed it on his head, with a reed in his right hand. And genuflecting before him, they mocked him, saying, "Hail, King of the Jews." (Matt 27:29)
Hail Mary…

And spitting on him, they took the reed and struck his head. (Matt 27:30)
Hail Mary…

After they had mocked him, they stripped him of the cloak, and clothed him with his own garments, and they led him away to crucify him. (Matt 27:31)
Hail Mary…

But as they were going out, they came upon a man of Cyrene, named Simon, whom they compelled to take up his cross. (Matt 27:32)
Hail Mary…

They arrived at the place, which is called Golgotha, which is the place of Calvary. And they gave him wine to drink, mixed with gall. And when he had tasted it, he refused to drink it. (Matt 27:33-34)
Hail Mary…

Then, after they had crucified him, they divided his garments, casting lots, in order to fulfill what was spoken by the prophet, saying: "They divided my garments among them, and over my vestment they cast lots." (Matt 27:35)
Hail Mary…

But those passing by blasphemed him, shaking their heads and saying: "Ah, so you would destroy the temple of God and in three days rebuild it! Save your own self. If you are the Son of God, descend from the cross." (Matt 27:39-40)
Hail Mary…

Similarly, the leaders of the priests, with the scribes and the elders, mocking him, said: "He saved others; he cannot save himself. If he is the King of Israel, let him descend now from the cross, and we will believe in him." (Matt 27:41-42)

Hail Mary...

"He trusted in God; so now, let God free him, if he wills him. For he said, 'I am the Son of God.'" Then, the robbers who were crucified with him also reproached him with the very same thing. (Matt 27:43-44)

Hail Mary...

Glory Be...

Decade 5

Our Father...

Now from the sixth hour, there was darkness over the entire earth, even until the ninth hour. (Matt 27:45)

Hail Mary...

About the ninth hour, Jesus cried out with a loud voice, saying: "Eli, Eli, lamma sabacthani?" that is, "My God, My God, why have you forsaken me?" (Matt 27:46)

Hail Mary...

Then certain ones who were standing and listening there said, "This man calls upon Elijah. "And one of them, running quickly, took a sponge and filled it with vinegar, and he set it on a reed, and he gave it to him to drink. (Matt 27:47-48)

Hail Mary...

Yet truly, the others said, "Wait. Let us see whether Elijah will come to free him." Then Jesus, crying out again with a loud voice, gave up his life. (Matt 27:49-50)

Hail Mary...

Behold, the veil of the temple was torn into two parts, from top to bottom. And the earth was shaken, and the rocks were split apart. (Matt 27:51)
Hail Mary...

The tombs were opened. And many bodies of the saints, which had been sleeping, arose. And going out from the tombs, after his resurrection, they went into the holy city, and they appeared to many. (Matt 27:52-53)
Hail Mary...

Now the centurion and those who were with him, guarding Jesus, having seen the earthquake and the things that were done, were very fearful, saying: "Truly, this was the Son of God."(Matt 27:54)
Hail Mary...

In that place, there were many women, at a distance, who had followed Jesus from Galilee, ministering to him. Among these were Mary Magdalene and Mary the mother of James and Joseph, and the mother of the sons of Zebedee. (Matt 27:55-56)
Hail Mary...

When evening had arrived, a certain wealthy man from Arimathea, named Joseph, arrived, who himself was also a disciple of Jesus. This man approached Pilate and asked for the body of Jesus. Then Pilate ordered the body to be released. (Matt 27:57-58)
Hail Mary...

And Joseph, taking the body, wrapped it in a clean finely woven linen cloth, and he placed it in his own new tomb, which he had hewn out of a rock. And he rolled a great stone to the door of the tomb, and he went away. (Matt 27:59-60)
Hail Mary...

Glory Be...

Passion Rosary II

According to the Gospel of John

Decade 1

Our Father

When Jesus had said these things, he departed with his disciples across the valley of Kidron, where there was a garden, into which he entered with his disciples. But Judas, who betrayed him, also knew the place, for Jesus had frequently met with his disciples there. (Jn 18:1-2)
Hail Mary…

Then Judas, when he had received a cohort from both the high priests and the attendants of the Pharisees, approached the place with lanterns and torches and weapons. And so Jesus, knowing all that was about to happen to him, advanced and said to them, "Who are you seeking?" (Jn18:3-4)
Hail Mary…

They answered him, "Jesus the Nazarene." Jesus said to them, "I am he." Now Judas, who betrayed him, was also standing with them. Then, when he said to them, "I am he," they moved back and fell to the ground. (Jn 18:5-6)
Hail Mary…

Then again, he questioned them: "Who are you seeking?" And they said, "Jesus the Nazarene." Jesus responded: "I told you that I am he. Therefore, if you are seeking me, permit these others to go away." (Jn 18:7-8)
Hail Mary…

Then Simon Peter, having a sword, drew it, and he struck the servant of the high priest, and he cut off his right ear. Now the name of the servant was Malchus. (Jn 18:10)
Hail Mary…

Therefore, Jesus said to Peter: "Set your sword into its sheath. Should I not drink the chalice which my Father has given to me?" (Jn 18:11)
Hail Mary…

Then the cohort, and the tribune, and the attendants of the Jews apprehended Jesus and bound him. And they led him away, first to Annas, for he was the father-in-law of Caiaphas, who was the high priest that year. (Jn 18:12-13)
Hail Mary…

Simon Peter was following Jesus with another disciple. And that disciple was known to the high priest, and so he entered with Jesus into the court of the high priest. (Jn 18:15)
Hail Mary…

The woman servant keeping the door said to Peter, "Are you not also among the disciples of this man?" He said, "I am not." (Jn 18:17)
Hail Mary…

Then the high priest questioned Jesus about his disciples and about his doctrine. Jesus responded to him: "I have spoken openly to the world. I have always taught in the synagogue and in the temple, where all the Jews meet. And I have said nothing in secret. Why do you question me? Question those who heard what I said to them. Behold, they know these things that I have said." (Jn 18:19-21)
Hail Mary…

Glory Be…

Decade 2

Our Father

Then, when he had said this, one of the attendants standing nearby struck Jesus, saying: "Is this the way you answer the high priest?" (Jn 18:22)
Hail Mary...

Jesus answered him: "If I have spoken wrongly, offer testimony about the wrong. But if I have spoken correctly, then why do you strike me?" And Annas sent him bound to Caiaphas, the high priest. (Jn 18:23-24)
Hail Mary...

Now Simon Peter was standing and warming himself. Then they said to him, "Are you not also one of his disciples?" He denied it and said, "I am not." (Jn 18:25)
Hail Mary...

One of the servants of the high priest (a relative of him whose ear Peter had cut off) said to him, "Did I not see you in the garden with him?" Therefore, again, Peter denied it. And immediately the rooster crowed. (Jn 18:26-27)
Hail Mary...

Then they led Jesus from Caiaphas into the praetorium. Now it was morning, and so they did not enter into the praetorium, so that they would not be defiled, but might eat the Passover. (Jn 18:28)
Hail Mary...

Therefore, Pilate went outside to them, and he said, "What accusation are you bringing against this man?" They responded and said to him, "If he were not an evil-doer, we would not have handed him over to you." (Jn 18:29-30)
Hail Mary...

Pilate said to them, "Take him yourselves and judge him according to your own law." Then the Jews said to him, "It is not lawful for us to execute anyone." This was so that the word of Jesus would be fulfilled, which he spoke signifying what kind of death he would die. (Jn 18:31-32)
Hail Mary...

Then Pilate entered the headquarters again, and he called Jesus and said to him, "You are the king of the Jews?" Jesus responded, "Are you saying this of yourself, or have others spoken to you about me?" (Jn 18:33-34)
Hail Mary…

Pilate responded: "Am I a Jew? Your own nation and the high priests have handed you over to me. What have you done?" (Jn 18:35)
Hail Mary…

Jesus responded: "My kingdom is not of this world. If my kingdom were of this world, my ministers would certainly strive so that I would not be handed over to the Jews. But my kingdom is not from this world." (Jn 18:36)
Hail Mary…

Glory Be…

Decade 3

Our Father

Pilate said to him, "You are a king, then?" Jesus answered, "You are saying that I am a king. For this I was born, and for this I came into the world: so that I may offer testimony to the truth. Everyone who is of the truth hears my voice." (Jn 18:37)
Hail Mary…

Pilate said to him, "What is truth?" And when he had said this, he went out again to the Jews, and he said to them, "I find no case against him. (Jn 18:38)
Hail Mary…

But you have a custom, that I should release someone to you at the Passover. Therefore, do you want me to release to you the king of the Jews?" (Jn 18:39)
Hail Mary…

Then they all cried out repeatedly, saying: "Not this one, but Barabbas." Now Barabbas was a robber. (Jn 18:40)
Hail Mary...

Therefore, Pilate then took Jesus into custody and scourged him. (Jn 19:1)
Hail Mary...

And the soldiers, plaiting a crown of thorns, imposed it on his head. And they put a purple garment around him. And they were approaching him and saying, "Hail, king of the Jews!" And they struck him repeatedly. (Jn 19:2-3)
Hail Mary...

Then Pilate went outside again, and he said to them: "Behold, I am bringing him out to you, so that you may realize that I find no case against him." (Jn 19:4)
Hail Mary...

(Then Jesus went out, bearing the crown of thorns and the purple garment.) And he said to them, "Behold the man." (Jn 19:5)
Hail Mary...

When the high priests and the attendants had seen him, they cried out, saying: "Crucify him! Crucify him!" Pilate said to them: "Take him yourselves and crucify him. For I find no case against him." (Jn 19:6)
Hail Mary...

The Jews answered him, "We have a law, and according to the law, he ought to die, for he has made himself the Son of God." Therefore, when Pilate had heard this word, he was more fearful. (Jn 19:7-8)
Hail Mary...

Glory Be...

Decade 4

Our Father

He entered into the praetorium again. And he said to Jesus. "Where are you from?" But Jesus gave him no response. Therefore, Pilate said to him: "Will you not speak to me? Do you not know that I have authority to crucify you, and I have authority to release you?" (Jn 19:9-10)
Hail Mary…

Jesus responded, "You would not have any authority over me, unless it were given to you from above. For this reason, he who has handed me over to you has the greater sin." (Jn 19:11)
Hail Mary…

And from then on, Pilate was seeking to release him. But the Jews were crying out, saying: "If you release this man, you are no friend of Caesar. For anyone who makes himself a king contradicts Caesar." (Jn 19:12)
Hail Mary…

When Pilate had heard these words, he brought Jesus outside, and he sat down in the seat of judgment, in a place which is called the Pavement, but in Hebrew, it is called Gabbatha. Now it was the preparation day of the Passover, about the sixth hour. And he said to the Jews, "Behold your king." (Jn 19:13-14)
Hail Mary…

But they were crying out: "Take him away! Take him away! Crucify him!" Pilate said to them, "Shall I crucify your king?" The high priests responded, "We have no king except Caesar." (Jn 19:15)
Hail Mary…

He then handed him over to them to be crucified. And they took Jesus and led him away. And carrying his own cross, he went forth to the place, which is called Calvary, but in Hebrew it is called the Place of the Skull. (Jn 19:16-17)
Hail Mary…

There they crucified him, and with him two others, one on each side, with Jesus in the middle. (Jn 19:18)

Hail Mary…

Then Pilate also wrote a title, and he set it above the cross. And it was written: JESUS THE NAZARENE, KING OF THE JEWS. (Jn 19:19)
Hail Mary…

Then the high priests of the Jews said to Pilate: Do not write, 'King of the Jews,' but that he said, 'I am King of the Jews.' Pilate responded, "What I have written, I have written." (Jn 19:21-22)
Hail Mary…

Standing beside the cross of Jesus were his mother, and his mother's sister, and Mary of Cleophas, and Mary Magdalene. (Jn 19:25)
Hail Mary…

Glory Be…

Decade 5

Our Father

Therefore, when Jesus had seen his mother and the disciple whom he loved standing near, he said to his mother, "Woman, behold your son." Next, he said to the disciple, "Behold your mother." And from that hour, the disciple accepted her as his own. (Jn 19:26-27)
Hail Mary…

After this, Jesus knew that all had been accomplished, so in order that the Scripture might be completed, he said, "I thirst." (Jn 19:28)
Hail Mary…

And there was a container placed there, full of vinegar. Then, placing a sponge full of vinegar around hyssop, they brought it to his mouth. Then Jesus, when he had received the vinegar, said: "It is consummated." And bowing down his head, he surrendered his spirit. (Jn 19:29-30)
Hail Mary…

Then the Jews, because it was the preparation day, so that the bodies would not remain upon the cross on the Sabbath (for that Sabbath was a great day), they petitioned Pilate in order that their legs might be broken, and they might be taken away. (Jn 19:31)
Hail Mary…

Therefore, the soldiers approached, and, indeed, they broke the legs of the first one, and of the other who was crucified with him. But after they had approached Jesus, when they saw that he was already dead, they did not break his legs. (Jn 19:32-33)
Hail Mary…

Instead, one of the soldiers opened his side with a lance, and immediately there went out blood and water. (Jn 19:34)
Hail Mary…

For these things happened so that the Scripture would be fulfilled: "You shall not break a bone of him." And again, another Scripture says: "They shall look upon him, whom they have pierced." (Jn 19:36-37)
Hail Mary…

Then, after these things, Joseph from Arimathea, (because he was a disciple of Jesus, but a secret one for fear of the Jews) petitioned Pilate so that he might take away the body of Jesus. And Pilate gave permission. Therefore, he went and took away the body of Jesus. (Jn 19:38)
Hail Mary…

Now Nicodemus also arrived, (who had gone to Jesus at first by night) bringing a mixture of myrrh and aloe, weighing about seventy pounds. Therefore, they took the body of Jesus, and they bound it with linen cloths and the aromatic spices, just as it is the manner of the Jews to bury. (Jn 19:39-40)
Hail Mary…

Now in the place where he was crucified there was a garden, and in the garden, there was a new tomb, in which no one had yet been

laid. Therefore, because of the preparation day of the Jews, since the tomb was nearby, they placed Jesus there. (Jn 19:41-42)
Hail Mary...

Glory Be...

Suffering Servant Rosary

Scriptural Rosary based on Jesus' call to suffer for the sins of humankind

Decade 1

Our Father...

Isaac said to his father Abraham, "Father". And he answered, "yes, my son? "Behold, the fire and the wood are here," he said, "but where is the lamb for the sacrifice?" And Abraham said, "My son, God will himself provide the lamb for the sacrifice." (Gen 22:7-8)
Hail Mary...

My God, my God, why have you forsaken me? why are you so far from helping me, and from the words of my groaning? (Ps 22:1/ Ps 21:2)
Hail Mary...

All those who trouble me are in your sight; my heart has anticipated reproach and misery. And I sought for one who might grieve together with me, but there was no one, and for one who might console me, and I found no one. And they gave me gall for my food. And in my thirst, they gave me vinegar to drink. (Ps 68:21-22)
Hail Mary...

Just as they were astonished over you, so will his countenance be without glory among men, and his appearance, among the sons of men. (Is 52:14)
Hail Mary...

He will rise up like a tender plant in his sight, and like a root from the thirsty ground. There is no beautiful or stately appearance in

him. For we looked upon him, and there was no aspect, such that we would desire him. (Is 53:2)
Hail Mary…

He is despised and the least among men, a man of sorrows who knows infirmity. And his countenance was hidden and despised. Because of this, we did not esteem him. (Is 53:3)
Hail Mary…

Truly, he has taken away our weaknesses, and he himself has carried our sorrows. And we thought of him as if he were a leper, or as if he had been struck by God and humiliated. (Is 53:4)
Hail Mary…

He himself was wounded because of our iniquities. He was bruised because of our wickedness. The discipline of our peace was upon him. And by his wounds, we are healed. (Is 53:5)
Hail Mary…

We have all gone astray like sheep; each one has turned aside to his own way. And the Lord has placed all our iniquity upon him. (Is 53:6)
Hail Mary…

He was offered up, because it was his own will. And he did not open his mouth. He will be led like a sheep to the slaughter. And he will be mute like a lamb before his shearer. For he will not open his mouth. (Is 53:7)
Hail Mary…

Glory Be…

Decade 2

Our Father…

He was lifted up from anguish and judgment. Who will describe his life? For he has been cut off from the land of the living. Because of the wickedness of my people, I have struck him down. (Is 53:8)
Hail Mary…

He will be given a place with the impious for his burial, and with the rich for his death, though he has done no iniquity, nor was deceit in his mouth. (Is 53:9)
Hail Mary…

It was the will of the Lord to crush him with infirmity. If he lays down his life because of sin, he will see offspring with long lives, and the will of the Lord will be directed by his hand. (Is 53:10)
Hail Mary…

Because his soul has labored, he will see and be satisfied. By his knowledge, my just servant will himself justify many, and he himself will carry their iniquities. (Is 53:11)
Hail Mary…

Therefore, I will allot to him a great number. And he will divide the spoils of the strong. For he has handed over his life to death, and he was reputed among criminals. And he has taken away the sins of many, and he has prayed for the transgressors. (Is 53:12)
Hail Mary…

From that time Jesus began to show his disciples that he must go to Jerusalem, and suffer many things from the elders, the scribes, and the chief priests, and be put to death, and on the third day rise again. (Matt 16:21)
Hail Mary…

Behold, we are ascending to Jerusalem, and the Son of man shall be handed over to the leaders of the priests and to the scribes. And they shall condemn him to death. And they shall hand him over to the Gentiles to be mocked and scourged and crucified. And on the third day, he shall rise again. (Matt 20:18-19)
Hail Mary…

And many, upon hearing him, were amazed at his doctrine, saying: "Where did this one get all these things?" and, "What is this wisdom, which has been given to him?" and, "Such powerful deeds, which are wrought by his hands! Is this not the carpenter, the son of Mary, the brother of James, and Joseph, and Jude, and

Simon? Are not his sisters also here with us?" And they took great offense at him. (Mrk 6:2-3)
Hail Mary...

He began to teach them, that the Son of Man must suffer many things, and be rejected by the elders and by the chief priests, and the scribes, and be killed, and after three days rise again. (Mrk 8:31)
Hail Mary...

Behold, we are going up to Jerusalem, and the Son of man will be handed over to the leaders of the priests, and to the scribes, and the elders. And they will condemn him to death, and they will hand him over to the Gentiles. And they will mock him, and spit on him, and scourge him, and put him to death. (Mrk 10:33-34)
Hail Mary...

Glory Be...

Decade 3

Our Father...

They said, "Grant to us that we may sit, one at your right and the other at your left, in your glory." But Jesus said to them: "You do not know what you are asking. Are you able to drink from the chalice from which I drink, or to be baptized with the baptism with which I am to be baptized?" (Mrk 10:37-38)
Hail Mary...

All those in the synagogue, upon hearing these things, were filled with anger. And they rose up and drove him beyond the city. And they brought him all the way to the edge of the mount, upon which their city had been built, so that they might throw him down violently. (Luk 4:28-29)
Hail Mary...

For just as lightning flashes from under heaven and shines to whatever is under heaven, so also will the Son of man be in his day.

But first he must suffer many things and be rejected by this generation. (Luk 17:24-25)
Hail Mary...

Then Jesus took the twelve aside, and he said to them: "Behold, we are ascending to Jerusalem, and everything shall be completed which was written by the prophets about the Son of man. For he will be handed over to the Gentiles, and he will be mocked and scourged and spit upon. And after they have scourged him, they will kill him. (Lk 18:31-33)
Hail Mary...

The lord of the vineyard said: 'What shall I do? I will send my beloved son. Perhaps when they have seen him, they will respect him.' And when the settlers had seen him, they discussed it among themselves, saying: 'This one is the heir. Let us kill him, so that the inheritance will be ours.' And forcing him outside of the vineyard, they killed him. (Lk 20:13-15)
Hail Mary...

He was separated from them by about a stone's throw. And kneeling down, he prayed, saying: "Father, if you are willing, take this chalice away from me. Yet truly, let not my will, but yours, be done." (Luk 22:44-42)
Hail Mary...

He said to them: "How foolish and reluctant in heart you are, to believe everything that has been spoken by the Prophets! Was not the Christ required to suffer these things, and then enter into his glory?" (Luk 24:25-26)
Hail Mary...

Then he opened their minds, that they might understand the scriptures. And he said to them, "Thus it is written, that it was necessary for the Messiah to suffer, and to rise again from the dead on the third day. (Luk 24:45-46)
Hail Mary...

He was in the world, and the world was made through him, and the world did not recognize him. He went to his own, and his own did not accept him. (Jn 1:10-11)
Hail Mary…

Just as Moses lifted up the serpent in the desert, so also must the Son of man be lifted up, so that whoever believes in him may not perish, but may have eternal life. (Jn 3:14-15)
Hail Mary…

Glory Be…

Decade 4

Our Father…

Jesus said to Peter: "Set your sword into its sheath. Should I not drink the chalice which my Father has given to me?" (Jn 18:11)
Hail Mary…

Then Paul, according to custom, entered to them. And for three Sabbaths he disputed with them about the Scriptures, interpreting and concluding that it was necessary for the Christ to suffer and to rise again from the dead, and that "This is the Jesus Christ, whom I am announcing to you." (Acts 17:2-3)
Hail Mary…

For God made him who did not know sin to be sin for us, so that we might become the justice of God in him. (2 Cor 5:21)
Hail Mary…

Christ has redeemed us from the curse of the law, since he became a curse for us. For it is written: "Cursed is anyone who hangs from a tree." (Gal 3:13)
Hail Mary…

We understand that Jesus, who was reduced to a little less than the Angels, was crowned with glory and honor because of his passion and death, in order that, by the grace of God, he might taste death for all. (Heb 2:9)

Hail Mary…

It was fitting for God, for whom are all things, and by whom are all things, who had brought many children into glory, to make the author of their salvation, perfect through sufferings. (Heb 2:10)
Hail Mary…

It is Christ who, in the days of his flesh, with a strong cry and tears, offered prayers and supplications to the One who was able to save him from death, and who was heard because of his reverence. And although, certainly, he is the Son of God, he learned obedience by the things that he suffered. (Heb 5:7-8)
Hail Mary…

Let us gaze upon Jesus, as the Author and perfecter of our faith, who, having joy laid out before him, endured the cross, disregarding the shame, and who now sits at the right hand of the throne of God. (Heb 12:2)
Hail Mary…

So then, meditate upon him who endured such adversity from sinners against himself, so that you may not become weary, failing in your souls. (Heb 12:3)
Hail Mary…

You have been called to this because Christ also suffered for us, leaving you an example, so that you would follow in his footsteps. He committed no sin, neither was deceit found in his mouth. (1 Pet 2:21-22)
Hail Mary…

Glory Be…

Decade 5

Our Father…

When he was reviled, he did not revile back: when he suffered, he did not threaten; but placed his hope in God who judges righteously. (1 Pet 2:23)

Hail Mary...

He himself bore our sins in his body upon the tree, so that we, having died to sin, would live for justice. By his wounds, you have been healed. (1 Pet 2:24)
Hail Mary...

It is better to suffer for doing good, if it is the will of God, than for doing evil. For Christ also died once for our sins, the Just One on behalf of the unjust, so that he might offer us to God, having died, certainly, in the flesh, but having been enlivened by the Spirit. (1 Pet 3:17-18)
Hail Mary...

The leaders of the priests, mocking him with the scribes, said to one another: "He saved others. He is not able to save himself. Let the Christ, the king of Israel, descend now from the cross, so that we may see and believe." Those who were crucified with him also insulted him. (Mrk 15:31-32)
Hail Mary...

I have given my body to those who strike me, and my cheeks to those who plucked them. I have not averted my face from those who rebuked me and who spit on me. (Is 50:6)
Hail Mary...

I am poured out like water; and all my bones are scattered. My heart is become like wax melting within me. My strength is dried up like a potsherd, and my tongue has cleaved to my jaws; and you have brought me to the dust of death. (Ps 22:14-15, Ps 21:15-16)
Hail Mary...

For many dogs have encompassed me: a company of evildoers have encircled me. They have dug my hands and feet. I can count my bones. And they have looked and stared upon me. (Ps 22:16-17, Ps 21:17-18)
Hail Mary...

I will pour out upon the house of David and upon the inhabitants of Jerusalem, the spirit of grace and of prayers. And they will look upon me, whom they have pierced, and they will mourn for Him as one mourns for an only son, and they will feel sorrow over him, as one would be sorrowful at the death of a firstborn. (Zech 12:10)
Hail Mary…

Come to the Lord, a living stone rejected by people, but chosen and honored by God. (1 Pet 2:4)
Hail Mary…

He humbled himself, becoming obedient even unto death, even the death of the Cross. (Phil 2:8)
Hail Mary…

Glory Be…

The Sorrowful Mysteries

Decade 1 (The Agony in the Garden)

Our Father...

Then Jesus went with them to a garden, which is called Gethsemane. And he said to his disciples, "Sit down here, while I go there and pray." (Matt 26:36)
Hail Mary...

Taking with him Peter and the two sons of Zebedee, he began to be sorrowful and saddened. (Matt 26:37)
Hail Mary...

Then he said to them: "My soul is sorrowful, even unto death. Stay here and keep vigil with me." (Matt 26:38)
Hail Mary...

Continuing on a little further, he fell prostrate on his face, praying and saying: "My Father, if it is possible, let this chalice pass away from me. Yet truly, let it not be as I will, but as you will." (Matt 26:39)
Hail Mary...

Again, a second time, he went and prayed, saying, "My Father, if this chalice cannot pass away, unless I drink it, let your will be done." (Matt 26:42)
Hail Mary...

And again, he went and found them sleeping, for their eyes were heavy. (Matt 26:43)
Hail Mary...

Leaving them behind, again he went and prayed for the third time, saying the same words. (Matt 26:44)
Hail Mary...

Then he approached his disciples and said to them: "Sleep now and rest. Behold, the hour has drawn near, and the Son of man will be delivered into the hands of sinners." (Matt 26:45)
Hail Mary...

Rise up; let us go. Behold, he who will betray me draws near. (Matt 26:46)
Hail Mary...

While he was still speaking, behold, Judas, one of the twelve, arrived, and with him was a large crowd with swords and clubs, sent from the leaders of the priests and the elders of the people. (Matt 26:47)
Hail Mary...

Glory Be…

Decade 2 (The Scourging at the Pillar)

Our Father…

Immediately in the morning, after the leaders of the priests had taken counsel with the elders and the scribes and the entire council, binding Jesus, they led him away and delivered him to Pilate. (Mrk 15:1-2)
Hail Mary...

Therefore, Pilate went outside to them, and he said, "What accusation are you bringing against this man?" (Jn 18:29)
Hail Mary...

They responded and said to him, "If he were not an evil-doer, we would not have handed him over to you." (Jn 18:30)
Hail Mary...

Therefore, Pilate said to them, "Take him yourselves and judge him according to your own law." Then the Jews said to him, "It is not lawful for us to execute anyone." (Jn 18:31)
Hail Mary...

Then Pilate entered the praetorium again, and he called Jesus and said to him, "You are the king of the Jews?" (Jn 18:33)
Hail Mary...

Jesus responded, "Are you saying this of yourself, or have others spoken to you about me?" (Jn 18:34)
Hail Mary...

Pilate responded: "Am I a Jew? Your own nation and the high priests have handed you over to me. What have you done?" (Jn 18:35)
Hail Mary...

Jesus responded: "My kingdom is not of this world. If my kingdom were of this world, my ministers would certainly strive so that I would not be handed over to the Jews. But my kingdom is not now from here." (Jn 18:36-37)
Hail Mary...

So Pilate said to him, "You are a king, then?" Jesus answered, "You are saying that I am a king. For this I was born, and for this I came into the world: so that I may offer testimony to the truth. Everyone who is of the truth hears my voice." Pilate said to him, "What is truth?" And when he had said this, he went out again to the Jews, and he said to them, "I find no case against him. (Jn 18:37-38)
Hail Mary...

Therefore, Pilate then took Jesus into custody and scourged him. (Jn 19:1)
Hail Mary...

Glory Be...

Decade 3 (The Crowning with the Thorns)

Our Father...

Then the soldiers led him away to the court of the praetorium. And they called together the entire cohort. (Mrk 15:16)
Hail Mary...

They clothed him with purple. And platting a crown of thorns, they placed it on him. (Mrk 15:17)
Hail Mary...

And stripping him, they put a scarlet cloak around him. (Matt 27:28-29)
Hail Mary...

Plaiting a crown of thorns, they placed it on his head, with a reed in his right hand. And genuflecting before him, they mocked him, saying, "Hail, King of the Jews." (Matt 27:29)
Hail Mary...

And spitting on him, they took the reed and struck his head. (Matt 27:30)
Hail Mary...

And they began to salute him: "Hail, king of the Jews." (Mrk 15:18)
Hail Mary...

And they struck his head with a reed, and they spit on him. And kneeling down, they reverenced him. (Mrk 15:19)
Hail Mary...

Then Pilate went outside again, and he said to them: "Behold, I am bringing him out to you, so that you may realize that I find no case against him." (Then Jesus went out, bearing the crown of thorns and the purple garment.) And he said to them, "Behold the man." (Jn 19:4-5)
Hail Mary...

But they were crying out: "Take him away! Take him away! Crucify him!" (Jn 19:15)
Hail Mary...

Pilate said to them, "Shall I crucify your king?" The high priests responded, "We have no king except Caesar."(Jn 19:15)
Hail Mary...

Glory Be…

Decade 4 (The Carrying of the Cross)

Our Father...

Therefore, he then handed him over to them to be crucified. And they took Jesus and led him away. (Jn 19:16)
Hail Mary...

After they had mocked him, they stripped him of the purple, and they clothed him in his own garments. And they led him away, so that they might crucify him. (Mrk 15:20)
Hail Mary...

Carrying his own cross, he went forth to the place, which is called Calvary, but in Hebrew it is called the Place of the Skull. (Jn 19:17)
Hail Mary...

They compelled a certain passerby, Simon the Cyrenian, who was arriving from the countryside, the father of Alexander and Rufus, to take up his cross. (Mrk 15:21)
Hail Mary...

Then a great crowd of people followed him, with women who were mourning and lamenting him. (Luk 23:27)
Hail Mary...

But Jesus, turning to them, said: "Daughters of Jerusalem, do not weep over me. Instead, weep over yourselves and over your children." (Luk 23:28)
Hail Mary...

For behold, the days will arrive in which they will say, 'Blessed are the barren, and the wombs that have not borne, and the breasts that have not nursed.' (Luk 23:29)
Hail Mary...

They led him through to the place called Golgotha, which means, 'the Place of Calvary.' And they gave him wine with myrrh to drink. But he did not accept it. (Mrk 15:22-23)
Hail Mary...

Then he said to everyone: "If anyone is willing to come after me: let him deny himself, and take up his cross every day, and follow me." (Luk 9:23)
Hail Mary...

For whoever will have saved his life, will lose it. Yet whoever will have lost his life for my sake, will save it. (Luk 9:24)
Hail Mary...

Glory Be...

Decade 5 (The Crucifixion)

Our Father...

When they arrived at the place that is called Calvary, they crucified him there, with the robbers, one to the right and the other to the left. (Luk 23:33)
Hail Mary...

Then Jesus said, "Father, forgive them. For they know not what they do." And truly, dividing his garments, they cast lots. (Luk 23:34)
Hail Mary...

The passersby blasphemed him, shaking their heads and saying, "Ah, you who would destroy the temple of God, and in three days rebuild it, save yourself by descending from the cross." (Mrk 15:29-30)
Hail Mary...

One of those robbers who were hanging blasphemed him, saying, "If you are the Christ, save yourself and us." (Luk 23:39)
Hail Mary...

But the other responded by rebuking him, saying: "Do you have no fear of God, since you are under the same condemnation?" (Luk 23:40)
Hail Mary...

Jesus said to him, "Amen I say to you, this day you shall be with me in Paradise." (Luk 23:43)
Hail Mary...

Standing beside the cross of Jesus were his mother, and his mother's sister, and Mary of Cleophas, and Mary Magdalene. Therefore, when Jesus had seen his mother and the disciple whom he loved standing near, he said to his mother, "Woman, behold your son." (Jn 19:25-26)
Hail Mary...

Now it was nearly the sixth hour, and a darkness occurred over the entire earth, until the ninth hour. (Luk 23:44)
Hail Mary...

Then Jesus, crying out again with a loud voice, gave up his life. (Matt 27:50)
Hail Mary...

Behold, the veil of the temple was torn into two parts, from top to bottom. And the earth was shaken, and the rocks were split apart. (Matt 27:51)
Hail Mary...

Glory Be...

More Titles from Gifted Books and Media

RETURN TO GOD
Confession Handbook

PREACHER'S HANDBOOK

SCRIPTURAL ROSARY
1000 Bible Verses

GOD'S PROMISES AND BLESSINGS
FOR AN ABUNDANT LIFE

30 REASONS TO GO TO CONFESSION

EXAMINATION OF CONSCIENCE
For Teens

FREEDOM FROM PORN
AND MASTURBATION

EXAMINATION OF CONSCIENCE
For Adults

EUCHARISTIC ADORATION
*Prayers, Devotions, and
Meditations*

GODLY CHILD
*Children's Guide to
Catholic Living*

EXAMINATION OF CONSCIENCE
For Children

TO JESUS WITH MARY
*Scriptural Rosary on the Life and
Ministry of Jesus*

Now on Sale
Available in Paperback and Ebook
www.giftedbookstore.com

DOWNLOAD THE APP AND PRAY ON THE GO

SCRIPTURAL STATIONS

AVAILABLE NOW

Made in the USA
Las Vegas, NV
11 March 2025

19381413R00056